THE WORLD'S MOST AMAZING
PLANET EARTH FACTS
For Kids

First published in Great Britain in 2002 by
Dean, an imprint of Egmont Books Limited,
239 Kensington High Street,
London W8 6SA

Copyright © 2002 Egmont Books Limited

ISBN 0 603 56062 8

1 3 5 7 9 10 8 6 4 2

Printed and bound in the U.A.E.

THE WORLD'S MOST AMAZING
PLANET EARTH FACTS
For Kids

Written and Compiled by: Guy Campbell & Mark Devins
Illustrated by: Paul Moran & Simon Ecob

There are more than 600 million telephone lines in the world today, yet almost half the planet's population has never made a phone call.

The famous explorer Captain Cook didn't think much of Hawaii and its legendary hospitality. Shortly after he got there, the natives killed him.

The breed of dog known as a Chow has a blue tongue and gets its name from the Chinese word for food. Why? Because it is so tasty to eat!

One airline, Virgin Atlantic Airways, discovered that it takes in an average of 13 pence per passenger per flight in loose change found stuck in the plane's seats. If that average was the same on all the flights worldwide, it would add up to £40 million a year!

Around one million kilos of doggy poo are deposited on the pavements of Britain every single day.

Amazon tribes have an unusual way of dealing with passing tarantulas. They barbecue them and eat them. Apparently they taste like prawns.

China has more people in it than any other country on Earth, well over a billion. One person in five alive today is Chinese.

The Pacific Ocean is very nearly as big as all the other oceans in the world put together. In some parts, the Pacific Ocean reaches depths of nearly 11,000 metres.

The American Government has 7.43 billion grams of gold tucked away for a rainy day. It is worth about 100.000.000,000 dollars (62.5 billion pounds sterling).

Big Ben, the bell in the Houses of Parliament clock tower in London, has been heard by more people than any other bell in the world.

In ancient Egypt, the hours were longer in the summer than in the winter months.

Chevrolet tried marketing a Chevrolet Nova in Spanish-speaking countries - it didn't sell well because NOVA means "doesn't go" in Spanish.

In the 1940s, the name of Bich pen was changed to Bic for fear that Americans would pronounce it 'Bitch.'

Ivanov is the most common Russian surname.

Native speakers of Japanese learn Spanish more easily than English. Native speakers of English learn Spanish more easily than Japanese.

The word fez is Turkish for hat.

The biggest palace on Earth is the Imperial Palace in Beijing. Building started in 1402. It is so huge that you could sleep in a different room every night for 25 years.

A hamlet is a village without a church; a town is not a city until it has a cathedral.

In Colombia, tapping the underside of the elbow with the fingers of the other hand suggests that someone is a little mean with their money. In Holland to signal that someone is a bit cheap, you would rub your nose with your forefinger from the top in a downward motion.

In Papua New Guinea, there are villages within five miles of each other in which different languages are spoken.

Every minute 47 bibles are sold or distributed throughout the world.

There are only 12 letters in the Hawaiian alphabet.

If the population of China walked past you in single file, the line would never end because of the new Chinese people being born.

The bigger the raindrops, the brighter the rainbow will be, and the sharper the difference between the colours.

The Tube, or London Underground rail system, is the world's biggest, with 408 kilometres of track. Over 700 million journeys are made on the Tube every year, and it has 270 stations. The record for visiting all of these stations in the quickest time is 18 hours, 18 minutes, or one station every four minutes, set by Robert Robinson and Tom McLaughlin in October 1994.

Holland has the most bikes in the world. One bike per person is the national average with an estimated 16 million bicycles nationwide. An average of 51 cars a year accidententally drive into the canals of Amsterdam.

The largest single flower on Earth is the Rafflesia or "corpse flower". They can grow up to four feet across, and smell awful.

In 1872, Victoria Woodhall became the first woman to run for President of the United States.

In 1960, Sirimavo Bandaraneike became the first woman to be elected as a head of state. She became the president of Sri Lanka.

The Kiwi, national bird of New Zealand, can't fly. It lives in a hole in the ground, is almost blind, and lays only one egg each year. Despite this, it has survived for more than 70 million years.

There are more insects in one square mile of rural land than there are human beings on the entire earth.

The English term "cop" came from Constable On Patrol.

Although modern images of India often show poverty and lack of development, India was the richest country on earth until the time of British invasion in the early 17th century.

At their nearest point, Russia and America are less than four kilometres apart.

Because of heavy traffic congestion, Julius Caesar banned all wheeled vehicles from Rome during daylight hours.

Devon is the only county in Great Britain to have two separate coasts.

The oldest living thing in existence is a Bristlecone Pine tree in the White Mountains of California, aged 4,600 years old.

Hawaii officially became a part of the USA on June 14, 1900.

Quito in Ecuador, South America, is said to have the nicest climate in the world - the temperature rarely drops below 46 degrees Fahrenheit during the night, or rises above 72 degrees Fahrenheit during the day.

In 1973 two blind Peruvian soccer teams played a match using a ball filled with dried peas.

If a woman commits adultery in the Tupuri tribe of Africa, she is forced to wear a brass ring round her neck for the rest of her life.

Every major league baseball team in the USA buys about eighteen thousand baseballs each season.

Dissolved salt makes up 3.5 per cent of the ocean.

During most of the Earth's history, the North and South Poles have been free of ice.

The Channel Tunnel between England and France is the longest underwater and rail tunnel in Europe, and the second longest in the world behind Seikan in Japan.

Did you know…

…that in America it is against the law to ride a motorcycle while wearing a disguise?

If a statue of a person on a horse has both front legs in the air, the person died in battle; if the horse has one front leg in the air, the person died as a result of wounds received in battle; if the horse has all four legs on the ground, the person died of natural causes.

If you can see a rainbow you must have your back to the sun.

Every year in France there is a Thieves' Fair, where people are encouraged to try to steal things from the stalls - if they think they can get away with it.

In a normal lifetime an American will eat 200 pounds of peanuts.

Duffel bags are named after the town of Duffel, Belgium, where they were first made.

Australia is the only country that is also a continent.

Damascus, Syria, was flourishing a couple of thousand years before Rome was founded in 753 BC, making it the oldest continuously inhabited city in existence.

Disney World in Orlando, Florida, covers 30,500 acres (46 square miles), making it twice the size of the island of Manhattan, New York.

French was the official language of England for over 600 years.

The Atlantic Ocean is saltier than the Pacific Ocean.

In Elizabethan England the spoon was such a prized rarity that people carried their own folding ones to banquets.

Denmark has the oldest national flag in the world.

A United Nations survey showed that fewer British postmen are bitten by dogs than in any other nation.

Every year, Americans dispose of 1.6 billion pens.

Half the peanuts grown in America are used for peanut butter.

In 1778, fashionable women of Paris never went out in blustery weather without a lightning rod attached to their hats.

In Albania, nodding the head means no and shaking the head means yes.

In Atlanta, Georgia, it is illegal to tie a giraffe to a telephone pole.

In France, a five-year-old child can buy an alcoholic drink in a bar

Buzz Aldrin was the second man to set foot on the Moon. 'Moon' was also his mother's name before she married Mr Aldrin.

Canada's coastline is six times longer than that of Australia.

In 1500 B.C. in Egypt, a shaved head was considered the ultimate in feminine beauty. Egyptian women removed every hair from their heads with special gold tweezers and polished their scalps to a high sheen with buffing cloths.

In 18th-century England, women's wigs were sometimes four feet high. They were dusted with flour and decorated with stuffed birds, replicas of gardens, plates of fruit or even model ships.

A baby is born every seven seconds.

Since Hindus don't eat beef, the McDonald's in New Delhi makes its burgers from sheep.

Eggs are sold on bits of string in Korea.

Eskimos don't gamble.

Even very clever people use only about one per cent of the possible words in the English language when they talk to each other.

In eighteenth-century England, there was an employee in illegal gambling dens whose only job was to swallow the dice if there was a police raid.

India has 50 million monkeys.

There are nearly half a million sauna baths in Finland.

Crocodiles kill 2,000 people each year.

The French fry wasn't invented in France; its origin is probably Belgian. The "French" in French fries doesn't refer to its country of origin but to the way they are made. Food that is cut into strips is said to be "Frenched". Since French fries are strips of potato that have been fried, they became known as French fried potatoes, or "French fries".

40% of McDonald's profits come from the sales of Happy Meals.

A toothpick is the object most often choked on by Americans.

Abdul Kassem Ismael, Grand Vizier of Persia in the tenth century, carried his library with him wherever he went. The 117,000 volumes were carried by 400 camels trained to walk in alphabetical order.

Cinderella is known as Tuna in Finland.

In 1976, a Los Angeles secretary named Jannene Swift officially married a 50-pound rock. The ceremony was witnessed by more than 20 people.

Mexico once had three different Presidents in the space of 24 hours.

Milk from young coconuts was successfully used as blood plasma during World War II.

The biggest ship in the world is an oil tanker called Jahre Viking.

The world's stupidest domesticated animal is thought to be the turkey.

The Ottoman Empire once had seven emperors in seven months. They died of (in order): burning, choking, drowning, stabbing, heart failure, poisoning and being thrown from a horse.

Neil Armstrong stepped on the moon with his left foot first.

About 10 million people in the world share your birthday.

According to scientists, gold exists on Mars, Mercury and Venus.

African witch doctors send their patients a bill only if they expect them to live.

Because metal was scarce, the Oscars given out during World War II were made of wood.

The first competition in the world's first Olympic games, 776 B.C., was a foot race. The participants were all males, and ran in the nude.

The oldest word in the English language is "town".

The winter of 1932 was so cold that the mighty Niagara Falls froze solid.

The official name for the city of Bangkok, Thailand is "Krung thep mahanakhon bovorn ratanakosin mahintharayutthaya mahadilok pop noparatratchathani burirom udomratchanivetma hasathan amornpiman avatarnsa thit sakkathattiyavisnukarmprasit" or "Krung thep" for short, which translates as "City of Angels."

In China, the Kentucky Fried Chicken slogan "finger-lickin' good" was translated into the nearest equivalent in Chinese. It was "eat your fingers off."

The word for dog in the ancient Australian aboriginal language Mbabaran happens, coincidentally, to be 'dog'.

There are a thousand times more living things in the sea than there are on land.

There are more Irish people in New York City than in Dublin, Ireland; more Italians in New York City than in Rome, Italy; and more Jews in New York City than in Tel Aviv, Israel.

The country of Sweden has the most phones per person on Earth.

Did you know…

…that in Poland, an extra place is set at the dinner table in case a stranger comes to call?

The world's chickens lay around 400,000,000,000 eggs each year.

According to an old law, if you bring a raccoon's head to the town hall in Henniker, New Hampshire, you are entitled to receive ten dollars from the town.

On average, lightning causes about 83 deaths in the United States each year.

All thunderstorms produce lightning. Lightning often strikes outside of heavy rain and may occur as far away as ten miles from any rainfall.

The typical thunderstorm is 15 miles wide and lasts 20 to 30 minutes.

Nearly 1,800 thunderstorms are occuring at any moment around the world.

The Prime Minister's official London residence is at Number Ten, Downing Street. It is built on the site of an old brewery, and the last private person to own the house was called Mr Chicken.

The moon weighs 81 billion billion tons.

The raccoon derives its name from the Indian word meaning 'he who scratches with his hands'.

The Salvation Army's motto is 'Blood and fire'.

The ship, the Queen Elizabeth 2, should always be written as QE2. QEII is the actual Queen.

The biggest tree in the world is "General Sherman", a giant sequoia in California - 83m tall and 25m round.

The world's biggest forest is in Siberia. It covers over 17 million square kilometres.

In 1063 the River Thames froze over for 14 weeks.

The McDonalds at the SkyDome in Toronto, Ontario is the only one in the world that sells hot dogs.

The world's record for continuous pogo stick jumping is 41 hours.

There are an average of 178 sesame seeds on a McDonald's Big Mac bun.

Sea ice contains between a tenth and a hundredth as much salt as seawater. You can melt it and drink it.

The amount of water on Earth has remained the same since the planet was formed some 4,600 million years ago.

You can see the stars during the day from the bottom of a well.

Bolivia has two capitals.

Jamaica has more churches per square mile than any other country in the world.

The Angel falls in Venezuela are nearly 20 times taller than Niagara Falls.

In ancient Greece "idiot" meant a private citizen.

Bulgarians are the biggest yoghurt-eaters in the world.

Czechs are the biggest consumers of beer in the world.

When we think of Big Ben in London, we think of the clock. Actually, it's the bell.

There is a hotel in Sweden built entirely out of ice. It melts and is rebuilt every year.

People from Manchester are Mancunians.

The name Kangaroo came about when some of the first white settlers in Australia saw this strange animal hopping along and they asked the Aborigines what it was called. They replied with 'Kanguru', which in their language means 'I don't know'.

At one point, the Circus Maximus in Rome could hold up to 250,000 people.

It is 7,000,000,000 miles to Pluto and back.

The first written account of the Loch Ness Monster, or Nessie, was made in AD 565.

At the Lone Pine Koala Sanctuary in Brisbane, Australia, tourists can cuddle one of 130 koalas. Koalas cannot be cuddled for more than 30 minutes per day. They must also get every fourth day off. At Lone Pine, koalas are timed when they go to the koala-cuddling area.

At full speed, and assuming the track would allow it, Japan's Maglev train could travel from London to Edinburgh in about an hour and a half.

Pasta existed for thousands of years before anyone ever thought to put tomato sauce on it. The Spanish explorer Cortez brought tomatoes back to Europe from Mexico in 1519. Even then, almost 200 years passed before spaghetti with tomato sauce made its way into Italian kitchens.

To cook one billion pounds of pasta, you would need 2,021,452,000 gallons of water - enough to fill nearly 75,000 Olympic-size swimming pools.

Despite a population of over a billion, China has only about 200 family names.

When ocean tides are at their highest, they are called "spring tides". When they are at their lowest, they are call "neep tides".

Rome has more homeless cats per square mile than any other city in the world.

Canada has more doughnut shops than any other country.

The full name for Britain–The United Kingdom of Great Britain and Northern Ireland–is the third longest country name in the world.

It would take 80 Moons to equal the weight of the Earth.

The world's most expensive jam (or jelly) is called confiture de groselles. It is a redcurrant preserve from a 14th-century recipe made in the tiny French town of Bar-Le-Duc.

Canada has more lakes than the rest of the world combined.

Throughout the South Pacific, no building is taller than the tallest palm tree.

It has been estimated that the deep seas may contain as many as 10 million species that have yet to be discovered.

The tallest sand dunes in the world are in the Sahara Desert. A single dune has enough sand in it to bury the Eiffel Tower.

The United States produces 19 per cent of the world's rubbish.

Did you know...

...that on average, the Swiss are the richest people in the world?

Soccer is the most attended or watched sport in the world.

In 1975 Junko Tabei from Japan became the first woman to reach the top of Everest.

About 42,000 tennis balls are used in the Wimbledon Championship.

Canada is an Indian word meaning "Big Village."

99% of the matter in our solar system is contained in the Sun.

A quarter of Russia is covered by forest.

The volume of water contained in the Amazon river is greater than the water in the next eight largest rivers in the world combined.

An Israeli insult is to point down at the upturned palm of one hand with the forefinger of the other hand, implying that "grass will grow on my hand before the words you are saying come true!"

Migrating geese fly in a V-formation to conserve energy. A goose's wings churn the air and leave an air current behind. Each bird gets a lift from the current left by the bird ahead. It is easier going for all, except the leader, so geese are apt to take turns in front.

The word "Checkmate" in chess comes from the Persian phrase "Shah Mat," which means "The king is dead".

Pinocchio is Italian for "pine head."

The Amazon river carries as much water in one day as the Thames carries past London in a whole year.

The British spend more per person on music than the people of any other nation. Together they buy 7.2% of the world music market.

Sumerians invented writing in the 4th century BC.

The largest statue in the world is Mount Rushmore, where the heads of four United States Presidents are carved into the Black Hills near Keystone, Dakota. The heads are 18 metres (60 feet) tall.

The first daily broadcast was started by the BBC in November 1936.

When, in 1990, engineers digging a railway tunnel under the English Channel broke through the last dividing rock, Britain and mainland Europe were joined for the first time since the last Ice Age.

Residents of Torquay may be surprised to learn that Sabre-toothed Tigers used to hang out in the area. Teeth from these scary cats have been found in nearby caves. Also native to the West Country half a million years ago were bears, rhinoceros and woolly mammoths. And some very nervous squirrels...

In 1956, there was an iceberg in the South Pacific larger than Belgium.

In Bangladesh, kids as young as 15 can be jailed for cheating in exams.

In France, there's a town called Y.

In space, you cannot cry because there is no gravity to make the tears flow.

In the Caribbean, there are oysters that can climb trees.

In Bhutan, all citizens officially become one year older on New Year's Day.

Los Angeles and San Francisco become 2.5 inches closer together each year because they are on opposite sides of the San Andreas fault.

Since 1934, Mexico City has sunk 26ft, an average of 4.6 inches a year.

The French-speaking residents of Belgium are called Walloons.

If you told someone that they were one in a million, you'd be saying there were 1,800 of them in China.

The Sun is 330,300 times bigger than planet Earth.

A full grown oak tree, during the typical growing season, gives off 28,000 gallons of moisture.

Mount Everest was named after Sir George Everest who was the Surveyor-general of India from 1830 to 1840. He was the first person to survey the peak's height accurately.

Fishing is the biggest participant sport in the world.

The oldest continuous trophy in sports is the America's Cup in sailing. It started in 1851, with Americans winning for a straight 132 years until Australia took the Cup in 1983.

Rainbows are most frequent in the early morning and late afternoon.

All gondolas in Venice, Italy must be painted black, unless they belong to a high official.

All American astronauts must be under six feet tall.

Only five countries in Europe touch only one other: Portugal, Denmark, San Marino, the Vatican City, and Monaco.

In India and Bangladesh, people discovered that tigers always attack people from behind. Face masks were invented to wear on the back of the head to confuse the hungry cats, and they worked.

The magician's words "hocus-pocus" are taken from the name of a mythological sorcerer, Ochus Bochus, who appears in Norse folk tales and legends.

Did you know...

...that the Pacific Salmon swims 2,500 miles back to its birthplace every year?

Oak trees do not have acorns until they are 50 years old or older.

Seoul, the South Korean capital, just means "the capital" in Korean.

Soweto in South Africa was derived from SOuth WEst TOwnship.

The Boston University Bridge is the only place in the world where a boat can sail under a train travelling under a car driving under an aeroplane.

The English Channel gets 300mm wider every year.

People who live in Monaco are called as 'Monegasques'.

The international telephone dialling code for Antarctica is 67.

The first word spoken on the moon was "okay".

The first words spoken by Thomas Edison on his newly invented phonograph were "Mary had a little lamb".

According to town law, in York, it is perfectly legal to shoot a Scotsman with a bow and arrow (except on Sundays).

Did you know...

...that in Japan, it is possible to buy your underwear from a machine in the street?

The fastest moon in our solar system circles Jupiter once every seven hours - travelling at 70,400 miles per hour.

The German Bundestag, or Parliament, has 672 members and is the world's largest elected legislative body.

The only married couple to fly together in space were Jan Davis and Mark Lee, who flew aboard the Endeavour space shuttle in 1992.

The Philippines consist of 7,100 islands.

The Red Cross is called the Red Crescent in Arab countries.

The Sun travels at a speed of 155 miles per second, but it still takes 230 million years for it to complete a single revolution of the galaxy.

Approximately one third of the Earth's land surface is desert.

Tasmania has the cleanest air in the inhabited world.

The Amazon rainforest produces half the world's oxygen supply.

The average iceberg weighs 20,000,000 tons.

On a windy day, pollen can travel up to 500 miles.

The Eiffel Tower has 2.5 million rivets.

The number of births in India each year is greater than the entire population of Australia.

The first city in modern history to reach one million people was London.

The word "ozone" comes from the Greek "ozo" which means "I smell."

The world's highest city is Lhasa, in Tibet.

There were once hundreds of gold-mining labour camps in Arctic Siberia. An estimated three million Russian prisoners died working in them.

Two objects have struck the earth with enough force to destroy a whole city. Each object, one in 1908 and one in 1947, struck regions of Siberia. Fortunately, no-one was hurt either time.

A square mile of Amazon jungle can contain 3,000 different species of tree.

Earth's atmosphere is, proportionally, thinner than the skin of an apple.

The world's largest coins, in size and standard value, were copper plates used in Alaska around 1850. They were about a metre (3 ft) long, half a metre (about 2 ft) wide, weighed 40 kg (90 lb), and were worth $2,500.

The biggest crowd at a World Cup Final was 199,854. They watched Uruguay against Brazil in Rio de Janeiro in 1950.

Rio de Janeiro translates as "River of January".

The word Spain means "the land of rabbits".

The Aztecs were an ancient people from Mexico. They believed that the Sun would die if they didn't offer it human sacrifices. The victims of sacrifice were laid on an altar and had their hearts ripped out while they were still alive. The Aztecs used to keep the skulls of sacrificed people on specially-made racks to display them nicely.

Karaoke means "empty orchestra" in Japanese.

The Sahara Desert is expanding half a mile south every year.

The South Pole is colder than the North Pole.

The world's largest waterfall has been drowned by a dam. The lake created by the dam is so deep that the site of the falls is now just an underwater cliff. The Guaira Falls, on the Parana River between Paraguay and Brazil, had a maximum height of 114m (347 ft), and the amount of water flowing over them was more than double the flow of Niagara Falls.

When offering your Chinese host a gift, you should remember that it is a common custom in China to refuse a gift several times before accepting it; this is a matter of politeness.

Nine is considered the luckiest number worldwide.

Uluru, or Ayers Rock, in central Australia is 1.5 miles (2.5 km) long, a mile (1.6 km) wide and 1,143 feet (348 metres) high. It is the world's biggest rock, though it is getting slightly smaller every year.

The biggest waves are in the Pacific Ocean: they reach up to 34 metres high.

The remotest place in the world is in the Pacific Ocean at 47º30' South - 120º West. This point is 2,575 kilometres from the nearest land.

The word "Aloha" is used for both hello and goodbye in Hawaii.

The word "karate" means "empty hand".

The term "mayday" used for signalling for help (after SOS) comes from the French "M'aidez" which means "Help Me".

A **Siberian Tiger** is capable of eating 75 pounds of meat in one sitting: that's the equivalent of 300 Big Macs.

More than 1,000 different languages are spoken in Africa.

Oymyakon, Siberia, is the world's coldest village. Temperatures as low as -68 Centigrade have been recorded there, but 4,000 people still call it home.

The hedge maze in the garden of Hampton Court Palace near London has been growing for over three hundred years. It was designed in 1690.

In Japan it is illegal for anyone but the royal family to own a burgundy-coloured car.

Planet Earth actually rotated faster a hundred million years ago, making each year longer by roughly five days. 600 million years ago a year lasted 425 days. It is getting slower all the time.

Harry Ramsden's in West Yorkshire is the world's biggest and most famous fish and chip shop. They get through a tonne of chips and half a tonne of fish daily.

When cavemen first came to Britain it was during one of many Ice Ages. So much of the ocean water was taken up by glaciers that it was possible to walk to Britain from mainland Europe.

A balloon released into the jet stream weather system would take two weeks to travel completely around the globe.

Eighty per cent of all people hit by lightning are men.

On the Pacific island of Chuuk, local boys can make beautiful girls fall in love with them using a potion made from centipedes' teeth and stingrays' tails.

The biggest island in Europe is Great Britain. It is ten times smaller than Greenland, with just 216,777 square kilometres of land.

The world's newest island is in the Ha'apai group, part of Tonga. It was first spotted on June 6th 1995 and it popped up due to some heavy activity from underwater volcanoes.

Summer on Uranus lasts for 21 years - and so does winter.

In Japan, it was once fashionable for girls to tattoo a moustache on their lip.

The largest iceberg ever recorded was 335km (208 miles) long and 97km (60 miles) wide.

The Sun is 864,000 miles wide.

America once had a five-cent note.

In 1894 there were only four cars in America.

The world's first roller coaster opened in 1884 at Coney Island, New York. It was designed by Lemarcus Thompson, a former Sunday-school teacher.

There are more than 14,000 types of rice.

Did you know...

...that Mexico City is built on the site of the old Aztec capital city of Tenochtitlan?

The Moon takes up about the same amount of space as the Pacific Ocean.

Worldwide, about 40 square miles of land are transformed into desert every day.

About one tenth of the Earth's surface is permanently covered with ice.

At the equator the Earth spins at about 1,000 miles per hour.

The Earth, in its history, has been hit by at least one million meteors.

For every person on earth, there are 200 million insects.

Approximately every five seconds, a computer somewhere in the world gets infected with a virus.

A day is actually 23 hours, 56 minutes and ten seconds long. To make up for the missing minutes, we have a Leap Year every four years, when an extra day is added to February – the 29th.

A Jewish year can be as long as 385 days, or as short as 353 days, depending on the various fast days and festivals there might be.

New Year's Day used to be on 25th March. It was changed to January 1st in 1600 in Scotland, and in 1751 in England.

Japanese days of the week are named after things: the Sun, the Moon, fire, water, wood, metal and earth.

In 1750 there were about 800 million people in the world. In 1850 there were a billion more, and by 1950, another billion. Then it took just 50 years to double to 6 billion.

Nessie, the Loch Ness monster, is protected by the 1912 Protection of Animals Acts of Scotland. With good reason - Nessie is worth $40 million annually to Scottish tourism.

A supertanker full of oil can be worth over a hundred million dollars more than an empty one.

There are more than 23,000 black cabs (taxis) working in London.

The most children born from the same mother, at one time, were decaplets. Born in Brazil, in 1946, eight girls and two boys were delivered.

Every year, more than 60 million people visit France, a country with a population of 60 million people.

Off the coast of southern California, around 200 bison still roam on Catalina Island. They are descendants of a few that were brought there in the 1920s for a movie and were left there.

The Chinese invented kites, gunpowder, silk, porcelain, cannons, decimal currency and ink, which they invented a hundred years before paper. They also invented the wheelbarrow...

The Great Wall of China is 3,460 kilometres long. It was built over a period of two thousand years.

Poon Lim, a seaman with the British Merchant Navy, survived for 133 days on a raft when his ship was torpedoed in 1942. When his raft finally reached land after four long months, the plucky sailor was still able to walk ashore.

The people of the island of Tristan da Cunha in the South Atlantic live 2,435 kilometres away from their nearest neighbours. This makes them the remotest people in the world.

In Alaska, it is legal to shoot bears. However, waking a sleeping bear for the purpose of taking a photograph is prohibited.

A leaky tap can waste up to half a million pints of water in one year.

There are approximately 10 million species of living things on earth, and the number increases every day.

The Moon rotates about its own axis in 29.5 days...which is identical to the time it takes to complete its orbit around the Earth. As a result, the side of the Moon we see at night is always the same one.

China was the first country to introduce paper money in 812.

The US government mints more than 10 billion penny (one cent) coins each year. That's 35 for every person in the country.

A Boeing 747 airliner holds about as much fuel as 6,000 Mini Coopers.

More redheads are born in Scotland than in any other country in the world. Eleven per cent of its population has red hair.

Legendary escapologist Harry Houdini was the first man to fly an aeroplane solo in Australia.

Earth travels through space at 66,700 miles per hour.

Earth's oceans are an average of 2 miles deep.

It is a lot harder to learn how to write in Chinese than English, because there are no letters in Chinese, only words. Each word has its own symbol, and over 2,000 of them are used in everyday speech. It is the oldest written language surviving, dating back around 7,000 years.

If the Earth was the size of an orange, the Moon would be the size of a cherry.

The St Vincent Islands, which were off the west coast of Panama, and the Aurora Islands, once near the Falklands, have completely disappeared, covered by the rising ocean.

The word "corr" actually means "odd" in Irish.

All planets in our solar system are named after an ancient Roman god or goddess. Earth was named after Terra, the Roman goddess of the land.

Half the world's population is under 25 years of age.

Cuba is the only island in the Caribbean to have a railway.

Drivers in Bangkok have priority over pedestrians at all times.

Irish Euros have a harp in the centre.

Donald Duck comics were once banned in
Finland because he doesn't wear any pants.

**To wish someone good luck in Austria,
you must first make two fists
(with your thumbs tucked inside
the fists), and then pound them
slightly on a table.**

Did you know…

**…that it is illegal for pets in Ohio, America to
be out at night without lights?**

The largest painting on earth is a 116,000-square-foot whale mural, 11 storeys tall, and 1,028 feet (313 m) round, encircling the Long Beach Convention Center in California. It was painted by Robert Wyland.

More than two million Southern Fur Seals – 95 per cent of the world's population – crowd onto the shores of little South Georgia Island every summer.

King George I of England could not speak any English.

Icelanders consume more Coca-Cola per head than any other nation.

Taking the size of the population into account, Sweden is the country in which you are least likely to be murdered.

In Wales, there are more sheep than people.

The largest employer in the world is the Indian railway system, employing over a million people.

If you took all the urine the world produces in one day, it would take a full 20 minutes to flow over Niagara Falls!

A third of all the water we produce is used to flush the toilet.

The Great Pyramid of Cheops was originally designed to have windows.

The word LEGO comes from the Danish, "LEg GOdt", which means "play well".

Nearly a quarter of the population of Poland was killed in the Second World War.

The oldest known burning fire is an underground coal fire in New South Wales, Australia. This fire started over 2,000 years ago when lightning struck a huge coal seam at a point where it reached the surface of the earth. Today the fire is more than 500 feet underground, and is still slowly eating away at the coal.

If it were possible for the human voice to be carried naturally for great distances through the air, it would take 14 hours for a shout bellowed in Australia to be heard on the west coast of the USA.

Canada is the only country not to win a gold medal in the summer Olympic Games while hosting the event.

In 1973, Swedish confectionery salesman Roland Ohisson was buried in a coffin made entirely of chocolate.

Sharks eat about 40 people a year, mostly in the Indian Ocean off the coast of Indonesia and Australia.

The shortest scheduled airline flight is made between the island of Westray to Papa Westray off Scotland. The flight lasts two minutes.

The one place where a flag flies all day, never goes up or comes down, and does not get saluted, is on the Moon.

Internationally, "Baywatch" was the most popular TV show in history.

The biggest explosion the world has experienced in recent history was the eruption of Krakatoa, an island volcano in Indonesia. Dust from the eruption fell to earth 3,000 miles away ten days later.

The British flag is not called "The Union Jack": its actually called "The Union Flag". It's called the Union Jack only when out at sea on navy ships.

Because of spiritual beliefs about building called Feng Shui, most Chinese houses face south.

Mandarin, spoken by 810 million Chinese, is the most commonly spoken language in the world.

The biggest island in the world is Greenland, with a massive 2.17 million square kilometres of land.

Light can travel around the earth at its equator seven and a half times in one second.

There are 1,040 islands around Britain, one of which is the smallest island in the world: Bishop's Rock.

The quickest anyone has rowed across the Atlantic is 41 days. This record was won by New Zealander Phil Stubbs in 1997.

The most populated city in the world - when major urban areas are included - is Tokyo, with 30 million residents.

The Vatican is the world's smallest country, at 0,44 square km (0.16 square miles).

The US flag displays 13 stripes, one for each of the original 13 states.

The first man to go all the way round the world by sea was Ferdinand Magellan. Near the end of his epic journey, he and his crew ran out of food and had to eat the leather that held the sails to the mast.

More people speak English in China than in the United States of America.

The world's biggest bat, the Flying Fox of southern Asia, can't fly. It glides.

The right side of a boat was called the starboard side due to the fact that the navigators used to stand out on the plank (which was on the right side) to get a clear view of the stars. The left side was called the port side because that was the side that you put in on at the port.

The correct response to the Irish greeting, "Top of the morning to you" is "And the rest of the day to yourself".

Hawaii is home to the world's largest active volcano, Mauna Loa, which is 120km long and 4,170 metres high. Most of Mauna Loa is underwater, and the last time it erupted was in 1984.

London's Heathrow Airport handles more international passengers than any other: over 44 million pass through every year.

The Spanish word for Navy is "Armada".

Rainbows are seen as an arch or semi-circle, but passengers in aeroplanes flying between the sun and a shower of rain can sometimes see a whole rainbow, which forms a complete circle.

On Mount Wai-'ale-'ale, Kauai, Hawaii, it rains up to 350 days of the year.

A day is the time it takes the Earth to spin round once. A year is the time it takes the Earth to go round the Sun.

In Yuma, Arizona, during the day, it is sunny 90 per cent of the time.

Before there were jets, jet-lag used to be called boat-lag.

The Eskimo language has over 20 words to describe different kinds of snow.

The national anthem of Greece has 158 verses.

Children playing on a beach made the first discovery of a diamond in South Africa.

The "You Are Here" arrow on a map is called the IDEO locator.

The world's average school year is 200 days per year. In the US, it is 180 days, in Sweden 170 days, and in Japan it is 243 days.

The longest street in the world is Yonge Street, which starts in Toronto, on the north shore of Lake Ontario, and winds its way north then west to end at the Ontario-Manitoba-Minnesota border.

In 1989, Chamoy Thipyaso of Thailand was convicted of fraud in a Bangkok criminal court. She was sentenced to 141,078 years in prison.

Author Charles Dickens wrote (and slept) facing north, aligning himself with the poles of the earth.

Before the turn of the century, newspapers were called Tabloids, Chronicles, Gazettes, etc. Most had local stories, and far away stories were quite old, as it took a while for stories to travel. With the introduction of the teletype, stories could be broadcast widely and at speed. Several of the papers started carrying a section with stories from everywhere - North, East, West, & South - and that's why they are called NEWSpapers, and why news is called news.

Did you know…

…that the Vikings made it to America five hundred years before the Pilgrim Fathers?

In ninth-century Ireland, the Vikings imposed a "nose tax". If you didn't pay it, you had your nose cut off.

Henry III became King of England when he was only ten months old.

If we were to up-turn the Millennium Dome at Greenwich, London, it would take 3.8 billion pints of beer to fill to the brim.

The most common place name in Britain is Newton, which occurs 150 times.

More than 40 per cent of American households with children have guns.

The biggest tidal wave ever recorded struck the Island of Lanai, Hawaii, 105,000 years ago. The wave was so huge it left deposits of debris 375 metres up a local mountain.

Wolf packs could be found in all the forests of Europe, and in 1420 and 1438, wolves roamed the streets of Paris.

Among the shortest people in the world are the Mbuti Pygmies of the Congo River basin, where the men reach an average of 4 feet 6 inches tall.

Among the tallest people in the world are the Tutsi from Rwanda and Burundi in central Africa, with the men averaging 6 feet tall.

Based on population, Chinese Mandarin is the most commonly spoken language in the world. Spanish follows in second place, English is third, and Bengali is fourth.

On the wettest days in a rainforest, up to 10 inches (250 millimetres) of rain can fall.

The largest Olympic stadium ever built was Stadium Australia in Olympic Park, Sydney. It seats 110,000 people.

The longest trip in a pedal boat was by Kenichi Horie in 1988. He went from Hawaii to Japan, a trip of 4,660 miles.

All the land on the earth, plus a bit more, could fit into the Pacific Ocean.

Although the official language of India is Hindi, there are 14 regional languages that are officially recognised for conducting national affairs. In addition, there are approximately 170 other languages and over 500 dialects. Of the Indian population of over 548 million, only about a quarter understand Hindi.

The longest place name in Britain is in Wales: Llanfairpwllgwyngyllgogerychwyrndrobwllllantysiliogogogoch. It means St Mary's Church in the hollow of the white hazel near to the rapid whirlpool of Llantysilio of the Red Cave.

A storm officially becomes a hurricane when its winds reach 74 miles per hour (119 kph).

Over the last 150 years, the average height of people in industrialised nations increased by 10 cm (4 in).

More personal telephone calls are made on Mother's Day in the USA than on any other day in any other country.

One in ten people in the world live on an island.

In the US, murder is committed most frequently in August and least frequently in February.

In 1932, when a shortage of cash occurred in Tenino, Washington, USA, notes were made out of wood.

Disneyland's famous Sleeping Beauty castle
was originally meant for Snow White,
but Disney executives changed the name for
extra publicity when the Sleeping Beauty
movie was released soon after the
castle was completed.

The first product to have a barcode on its packaging was Wrigley's chewing gum.

Wrigley's promoted their new spearmint-flavoured chewing gum in 1915 by mailing four sample sticks to each of the 1.5 million names listed in US telephone books.

In 1980, there was a traffic jam stretching northwards outside Lyons in France that was 176 kilometres (109 miles) long.

China's Beijing Duck Restaurant can seat 9,000 people at one time.

The expletive, "Holy Toledo," refers to Toledo in Spain, which became a centre of Christian culture in 1085.

The Radio City Music hall cinema in New York, USA, has seats for 5,874 people.

Though rare in Britain, tornadoes are not unheard of. On 23rd November 1981, 58 were reported around the country.

In 1955 the richest woman in the world was Mrs Hetty Green Wilks, who left an estate of $95 million in a will that was found in a tin box with four pieces of soap.

There are more than seven million millionaires in the world.

If California was a country, it would be the fifth largest economy in the world.

Cumulonimbus clouds are the biggest. In tropical regions, these storm-bearing monsters have been measured at 20,000 metres high. That's 12.5 miles.

The Foxwoods casino in Connecticut, USA, has over 3,500 fruit machines.

A single share of Coca-Cola stock, purchased in 1919, when the company went public, would have been worth $92,500 in 1997.

The Cullinan Diamond is the largest gem-quality diamond ever discovered. Found in 1905, the original 3,100 carats were cut to make jewels for the British Crown Jewels and the British royal family's collection.

The Eiffel Tower receives a fresh coat of 300 tons of reddish-green paint every seven years.

When the Titanic sank after striking an iceberg on April 14th, 1912, 705 people survived the freezing waters to be rescued. These were largely the First Class passengers who were allowed to take all the lifeboats.

The world's largest alphabet is Cambodian, with 74 letters.

Flying from London to New York by Concorde, due to the time zones crossed, you can arrive two hours before you leave.

There are about 5,000 different languages spoken on Earth.

Did you know...

...that in March of 1911, the snow in Tamarac, California was 37 feet deep on the ground?

A rainbow is a trick of light caused by the sun passing through raindrops, breaking up the light into all the colours of the spectrum.

Sometimes a fainter, second, rainbow can be seen behind the first rainbow: if you look closely at the copy, you will notice that the colours are in the reverse order.

The best place in the world to see a rainbow is Honolulu in Hawaii. In the morning, or at sunset, the sky becomes quite orange and the rainbows, instead of being multicoloured, appear to be bright red.

Because of the difference in wind speed and direction, it always takes longer going to America across the Atlantic than it does coming back.

All pilots on international flights speak English, regardless of their country of origin.

221b Baker Street is one of London's most famous addresses. It was, of course, the home of Sherlock Holmes and his companion, Dr Watson. Hundreds of tourists every year still try and find it, but it doesn't exist.

Every year, the Moon moves a further 3.82cm from the Earth.

In the early history of the Earth, the Moon would have looked about three times larger in the sky, because it was closer to us.

The legendary voyager Captain James Cook made sure his crew got their necessary amounts of vitamin C on long voyages with carrot marmalade and huge jars of pickled cabbage.

There are more chickens in the world than people.

In the UK alone there are 30.6 million hens laying eggs.

The UK eats 807 million chickens every year.

The Silkworm Moth is the world's only completely domesticated insect. They are no longer found in the wild and have been cultivated by man for so long that they have forgotten how to fly.

85,000,000 tons of paper are used each year in America.

A notch carved in a growing tree will remain the same distance from the ground as the tree grows taller.

When the Eiffel Tower was built in 1884,
Parisians referred to it as
"the tragic lamppost".
It was nearly
universally hated.

The population of the entire world in 5000 B.C. was five million.

The sun's warming rays travel through 93 million miles of space to reach Earth. Moving at the speed of light, they make the trip in just eight minutes. A jet airliner would need more than 18 years to complete the same journey.

The cargo bay of a space shuttle is large enough to hold a Humpback Whale.

There are more than 10,000 golf courses in the United States.

The town of Calma, in the Atacama Desert in Chile, has never had rain.

Ten per cent of the world's men are left-handed while only eight per cent of women are left-handed.

The world's largest collection of human brains is in a bomb shelter beneath a psychiatric hospital in Essex. Eight thousand brains collected over the past 40 years are available for researchers to study.

When a Malaysian person stands with their hands on their hips, this is a sign of anger.

The Masai are one of the most famous of Kenya's many tribes. The Masai culture is totally based upon their cattle, and their diet consists of fresh and curdled milk, mixed with fresh blood tapped from the jugular vein of their cows.

The English are now the fattest people in Europe. Nearly 20% of England's population is officially classed as obese.

The average Briton consumes 35 times as much energy as the average Indian.

The deepest point in the sea—the Mariana Trench off Guam in the Pacific Ocean—is 6.77 miles (10.9 km) below sea level.

The Nullarbor Plain of Australia covers 100,000 square miles (160,900 km) without a single tree.

The national anthem of the Netherlands, Het Wilhelmus, is an "acrostichon". That means that the first letters of each of the fifteen verses represent the name Willem Van Nassov, who was king at the time it was written.

The Sanskrit word for "war" means "desire for more cows".

The globe-trotting Vikings used to remember some of the folks they met on their many travels by killing them and making cups out of their skulls.

Small flat icebergs have been fitted with sails and piloted more than 2,400 miles from the Antarctic to Peru.

The ancient Chimu people of Peru sewed gold to their clothes. A tunic was recently found with 13,000 pieces attached.

The biggest pumpkin ever was grown in Ontario, Canada by Herman Bax. It weighed in at a staggering 449 kilogrammes (990 pounds).

The most common name for a pet goldfish is "Jaws".

The most common name in Italy is Mario Rossi.

Blackpool in the north of England has a smaller proportion of native-born residents than any town in the world except Houston, Texas.

Canada has one-third of all the fresh water in the world.

In 1783, William Pitt the Younger became Britain's youngest Prime Minister at the age of 24 years, 205 days.

The Aztecs were great farmers, irrigating land and reclaiming it from lakes and seas to make fertile growing soil. They ate well too. Tomato, Avocado and Chocolate are all Aztec words.

The month of January is named after the Roman god Janus.

Did you know...

...there is a fortune in gold and jewels sunk in the Caribbean Sea?

The first words spoken by Alexander Bell over his newly invented telephone were: "Watson, please come here. I want you".

Hawaii is home to some of the best surfing in the world. In 1868, a native called Holua is believed to have surfed on a wave 15 metres (50 feet) high.

Bookkeeper and bookkeeping are the only words in the English language with three consecutive sets of double letters.

The longest place name still in use is: "Taumatawhakatangihangakoauauota mateaturipukakapikimaungahoronuk upokaiwhenuakitanatahu". It's a hill in New Zealand.

Queen Elizabeth I of England used to stuff her mouth with cloth to disguise the fact that she had no front teeth.

On Holy Wednesday, in villages of Lithuania, there was once the tradition of dragging a real herring around the local church. Today, children draw a picture of a herring on a flat board and drag that around the church instead. In the churchyard, the fish-draggers are followed by a crowd, all whipping the fish picture with sticks.

At Italian weddings, the bridegroom's tie is chopped into pieces and sold to the guests at the reception. The money raised is then put towards the happy couple's honeymoon expenses.

Direct eye contact is considered impolite in Japan. Folding your arms across your chest is a sign of arrogance and pride in Finland and is disrespectful in Fiji.
Crossing your fingers means good luck in America and in Europe, but is extremely rude in Paraguay.

The Guinness Book of Records holds the record for being the book most often stolen from British public libraries.

The Gulf Stream ocean current could carry a message in a bottle at an average of four miles per hour.

The expression "Son of a Gun" comes from the days when women were allowed to live in naval ships. The son of the gun was one born in the ship often in a space near the midship gun, behind a canvas screen. If the father's identity was uncertain, the child was entered in the log as "Son of a Gun".

Good old Saint Nicholas is not just the patron saint of children, but also of sailors, prisoners, perfumiers, unmarried girls and chemists. He is also Russia's national saint. He goes by many names around the world, including Sanctus

Nicolaus, Sint Klaes and of course, Santa Claus. He was born in the 4th Century and was the Bishop of Myra in Turkey. Legend has it that he rescued three sailors from a storm, three wrongly accused men from death, and three children from being pickled in a barrel.

PICKLES

About 3,000 stars are visible to the naked eye.

The number "four" in Japanese is considered unlucky because it is pronounced the same as the word for "death".

The Boeing Commercial Aeroplane factory in Washington is the largest building in the world. Disneyland, including car parks, could fit inside it.

The word Eskimo means "eater of raw flesh".

The Ark of the Covenant, sought by Indiana Jones in "Raiders of the Lost Ark" is said to be located in Axum, Ethiopia.

Sweden has the lowest birth rate in the world. Malawi, in Africa, has the highest.

Great Britain was the first county to issue postage stamps. Hence, the postage stamps of Britain are the only stamps in the world not to bear the name of the country of origin. However, every stamp carries a relief image or a silhouette of the monarch's head instead.

Dinosaurs were among the most sophisticated animals that ever lived on Earth. They survived for nearly 150 million years -- 75 times longer than humans have now lived on the planet.

The traditional greeting among members of the Maori tribes of New Zealand is to rub noses together.

China is, not surprisingly, the world's biggest producer of rice, but it also produces more potatoes, wheat, sheep, fish, cotton, iron and cement than any other country in the world.

A gesture particular to Portugal is used when you want to suggest that you have enjoyed your dinner and want to compliment the host or hostess on the meal. At the end of the meal, simply kiss the side of your index finger and then pinch your earlobe between the kissed index finger and the thumb.

Button-down collar shirts were invented by polo teams in England, to prevent their collar points from flapping about in their faces during vigorous riding.

In 1867, United States Secretary of State William H. Seward offered Russia $7,200,000, or two cents per acre, for Alaska. On October 18, 1867, Alaska officially became the property of the United States of America. Many Americans called the purchase "Seward's Folly".

Sharks lay the largest eggs in the world.

In Australia, Santa's sleigh is pulled by eight white kangaroos.

In Italy, on the evening of the day after Christmas, children are visited by a good witch named Strega Buffana. She flies around Italy on a broomstick and leaves treats for good children and coal for naughty ones.

In Norway, on Christmas Eve, a bowl of porridge, "nisse", is left in the barn for the gnome who protects the farm.

Texas was an independent nation from 1836 to 1845. The word Texas comes from the Hasinai Indian word "tejas" meaning "friends" or "allies."

In Peru, Inca Cola is more popular than Coca-Cola, and Scotland, Irn Bru is.

The most difficult language to learn is Basque, which is spoken in northwestern Spain and southwestern France. It is not related to any other language in the world and has an extremely complicated word structure and vocabulary.

In most languages, the sound "ma" is used to mean "Mother". In the Georgian language however, the word for mother is "deda", and father is "mama".

In Britain and Australia the light switch is turned down to switch on the light. In the United States the switch is turned up.

People in Iceland read more books than people anywhere else in the world.

The potato is originally from Peru. It was brought to Europe by the Spanish.

Every year towards the end of July a unique sporting event takes place in Fairbanks, Alaska. It is the World Eskimo Indian Olympics. The games are traditional competitions of the Eskimo and Indian people of Alaska. They include among other events: the Blanket Toss, Ear Pulling, One Footed High Kick, Two Footed High Kick and Knuckle Hopping.

In downtown Lima, Peru, there is a brass statue of Winnie-the-Pooh.

You would need 1,435,738 gallons of paint to cover the island of Bermuda.

In 1971 the United Nations declared that there were 576,100 tonnes of tea in China.

The largest pearl in the world was found in the Philippines. It is a size of a tennis ball.

The electron is the fastest thing in the world.

New Zealand was the first country in the world where women could vote.

The largest toy distributor in the world is McDonald's.

At latitude 60 degrees south you can sail all the way around the world without hitting land.

Did you know...

...that according to surveys, the snake is the world's least popular animal?

In Thailand, any person of other than Royal blood must crawl along the floor when in the presence of Royalty. Another person's head must never be higher than the King's or any other member of the family. The film "The King and I" has never been shown in Thailand.

The name Coca-Cola in China was first translated "Ke-kou-ke-la". Unfortunately, it was not discovered until after thousands of signs had been printed that the phrase means "bite the wax tadpole". Coke then researched 40,000 Chinese characters and found a close match, "Ko-kou-ko-le," which can be loosely translated as "happiness in the mouth."

Alaska has 29 volcanoes.

The Sun is 330,300 times larger than Earth.

If you enjoyed this book, you can find more hilarious jokes, amazing facts, and brainbusting riddles and puzzles in the following books, also published by Dean:

Title	ISBN
The World's Funniest Animal Jokes for Kids	0 603 56064 4
The World's Funniest Disgusting Jokes for Kids	0 603 56065 2
The World's Funniest School Jokes for Kids	0 603 56063 6
The World's Most Amazing Animal Facts for Kids	0 603 56060 1
The World's Most Amazing Science Facts for Kids	0 603 56061X
1000 of the World's Funniest Jokes for Kids	0 603 56066 0
1000 of the World's Most Astonishing Facts for Kids	0 603 56067 9
1000 of the World's Greatest Brainbusters	0 603 56068 7